Call Me Home

poems

Harman Kaur

central
avenue
2025

Published by Central Avenue Poetry, an imprint of Central Avenue Marketing Ltd.
www.centralavenuepublishing.com

CALL ME HOME

Trade Paperback: 978-1-77168-399-9
Epub: 978-1-77168-400-2

Published in Canada
Printed in United States of America

1. POETRY / Asian American   2. POETRY / Women Authors

3 5 7 9 10 8 6 4 2

For Subeg Singh,
I will never be home
without you.

The pain taught me how to write
and the writing taught me how to heal.

PART 1
Displaced

INTERGENERATIONAL PAIN

I learned silence from my father;
this is the only way he was ever allowed to grieve.

I inherited my mother's rage;
this is the only way she was ever heard.

NUMB

There is no doubt about it:
It is easier to think of anything but the grief,
to drift in a constant state of numbness.

The cuts keep coming, but I no longer feel them.
I wear my scars like badges, battle-worn,
yet, truth be told,
I do not remember when they formed—or how.

The anesthesia will fade, eventually,
but healing means confronting the pain.

And who wants to walk down the street,
only to come face to face with their mistakes?

THE ECLIPSE

If I told you
about the darkness
inside me,

would you still look at me
like I am the Sun?

CHEKHOV'S GUN

In another lifetime,

I learn not to carry the hurt
like a loaded gun.

In another lifetime,

you are bulletproof.

THE IMAGINED WOMAN

The men—
they want a good woman, modest,
wrapped from head to toe,
like a secret not to be revealed.

Yet the men—
they like to imagine,
with lustful paintbrushes
and hungry eyes.
Her body becomes their canvas,
where they paint picture after picture.

The men—
they do not know her secret,
but they are left satisfied,
all the same.

I CRY ON MY BIRTHDAY

It is October, again,
and I get hit with a sense of melancholy,
as I ponder another round around the sun,
with nothing to show for it.

Nothing has changed and
I desperately wanted things to be different by now.

It has been a long year.
I try not to think about the way that time evades me.

The days, they have dragged on, but they also
slip through my fingertips.

I can't remember what I did three days ago,
but it was probably nothing important.
I want to say that this year has not been kind to me,
but I know it is useless to complain.

I am alive, after all.
Sometimes, that is a comforting thought.
Other times, not so much.

Another year has passed me by.
I am alive.   That is all.

THE HAUNTING

One night, all the ghosts of my past appeared,
filling me with longing for what I had given up on
(for what had given up on me).

In a trance, I followed them,
my grip on reality loosening,
the weight of everything I had ever lost
lifting away.

I let myself linger there awhile,
amid loose ends and what-ifs.

I saw the bridges I had burned,
and there you stood—just as I remembered you.

I wanted to ask why you left,
but I knew if I stayed too long,
I might become a spirit myself.

What haunts me now is this:
Am I your ghost, too?
Or was I never even worth keeping as a memory?

AN EFFIGY FOR NOTHING IMPORTANT

I think I was supposed to be great.
Instead, I became a statue:
    unable to move forward,
too afraid to look back.

In some places,
they pray to beautiful
    sculptures of gods,
but no one leaves
    offerings at the feet of
someone who could have
    been great. No one visits
and it gets quite lonely.

IF GOD REALLY WAS AN OLD MAN

with a white beard
living in the clouds above,

I would point an accusatory finger
towards the heavens
and scream until my lungs gave out.

And maybe it would rain down on me,
the anger of a god,
but I would joyfully accept this as a sign that
I am not some forgotten thing
              among billions of others.

TENDER BEGINNINGS

I was too young when I discovered sorrow—
not the kind you feel when you fall and scrape your knee,
but the kind that seeps into your spirit,
stealing the sleep from your eyes.

No child should be made aware of their soul,
because once you know it exists,
you spend the rest of your life
trying to figure out how to save it.

TO BE UNDERSTOOD

My biggest mistake was needing you to understand
every part of my pain.
I wanted so desperately for you to see
why I am the way I am—
that wounds like mine do not just appear by magic.
I needed you to feel the violence that created them.

I begged you to understand,
but what I really meant was:

Please hold me while I figure myself out.

Please don't leave if it takes too long.

GOOD MOURNING

The mourning begins every day as soon as I open my eyes.
    Sunlight manages to filter in through
drawn curtains as the loss begins to set in,
and there is no way that I can stop it from
    peeking in on my suffering.

That damned sun!
It's always going to be there no matter what I do, isn't it?
I crave darkness. The light serves as a reminder that god exists.
The sun tries to baptize me.

    I crawl deeper under the covers.
Night comes and brings with it the promise that the sun will stop by
tomorrow.   And bring with it my pain.

THE CONFRONTATION

One night, I left home,
tracked down my perpetrator,
and tore him to shreds.

I burned down the houses of my enemies,
spray-painted my name
across the walls that had kept me out.

Triumphant, I returned home—
but what did I find?

My pain, waiting for me,
right where I had left it,
beckoning me to sit down
and talk.

THE FORGETTING

How tragic it is when a woman forgets:

That she, too, once woke to bloodstained sheets,
dumbfounded.
That she, too, once walked away from her father's house.
That she, too, once carried life inside her,
and brought that life into the world.
That she, too, once felt the throes of first-time motherhood.

That she, too, will always know:
To be a woman
is to spend a lifetime hiding your pain.

The greatest tragedy is not womanhood itself,
but knowing the anguish
and still choosing to inflict it on another.

The greatest tragedy is to forget.

LEAVING YOUR CHILDHOOD HOME

is bidding farewell to the little parts
that make up who you are,
whispering promises to visit often
and never forget.

Leaving your childhood home

is long, nostalgic trips down memory lane
from a country away,
punctuated by short, infrequent visits—
convincing yourself that next time will be longer.

Leaving your childhood home
is returning as a guest,
goodbyes masked by reassuring smiles
(I'm okay)
to hide the tears behind eyes longing for familiarity
(I'm breaking inside),
and embraces that are never long enough,
because they cannot last a lifetime.

LET'S BLAME GOD

for the heartbreak,
for the violence,
and for the wars.

Let's blame god for world hunger
and for starving children
and every despicable thing that befalls humans.

Let's blame god in every breath
until it becomes a sort of meditation,
and then maybe, just maybe,
we will be forgiven for our sins.

SECRET RAGE

I, like my mother, and her mother before her,
carry a secret rage inside me.

They say a woman is born with all the eggs
she will ever have,
formed while still inside her mother's womb.

I never met my maternal grandmother,
but I suppose I was there with my mother,
inside her,
and together, we bore witness
to the curse of womanhood.

Perhaps that is why we were both born angry.

MY BODY IS

a battleground
an auction
an amusement park
a court case
an incubator
a vessel for a man's honor
a work of art
a business deal
a punching bag
a comedy show
a tourist attraction

it is all these things, before it is mine

THE BIOLOGICAL CLOCK

The truth is, I do not know if I have what it takes to be a good mother. My friend tells me all you need to know about babies is how to feed them, bathe them, and keep them alive. The rest is all instinct, she says. *Don't overthink it.*

I do worry, though. I love getting the right amount of sleep too much. I have so many places I have yet to travel to. Social media floods me with doubts. *Focus on your career. Get all your travel plans out of the way.* I still have not seen the Eiffel Tower yet. Japan calls my name.

I will admit it, though. There is a desire within me I do not know how to quiet. To carry a child inside me. To bring it into this world. Call it hormones or nature. Call it whatever you want.

It is real and it exists.

Girls find out about the biological clock from a young age. Take your time, they tell us. *Tick tick.* Not too long, though. *Tick tick.*

Somewhere in the world, a woman cries in despair at yet another negative pregnancy test. *Tick tick.* It has been six years. *Tick tick.*

This is what it must mean to be a woman, I suppose. To always be in a race against our own bodies. *Tick tick.* To always be running out of time.

ANTICIPATORY GRIEF

will be the end of me. I imagine losing my parents. My dog.
I curse the natural order of life that requires me to live a portion of my life
without them.

I am afraid.

I do not think I can face all the hurt that life has in store for me.

I have anticipated this grief for so long that perhaps I will meet that pain
not as an enemy, but as an old friend. When it inevitably reaches my door,
I hope I can invite it in.

I hope I can thank it because great grief only exists where there was a
great love.

THEY TELL ME THAT THE TRAUMA WAS NECESSARY

I understand, truly. Life is meant to be a tapestry of lessons,
weaving us into better, stronger beings.

Yet, I assure you, I could have thrived without
such a deep, enduring wound. The child within me
might have blossomed, free from the weight
of pain carried into womanhood.

What I wish to say is this:
If only there existed a guide to reveal the lessons
that trauma left in its wake.
I did not need to suffer so intensely.

For as long as I did.

For as long as I am.

BLURRED LINES

We met. You asked me about love

and I described to you a deep hatred.

You laughed. *That is the opposite of love.*

I apologize. The line between the two has always been blurry for me.
I learned how to love whilst being starved. I lived off crumbs.

I get angry when I am left hungry for too long.

PANJAB

She is the land of five rivers
but Panjab is kept thirsty.

GLORIOUS LAND OF FIVE RIVERS

torn apart / borders hurt /

a sixth river / tears of mothers / blood of martyrs /

my people are thirsty / crops are thirsty /

there is not enough water /

for us / there is not enough water

THE TRUTH ABOUT HEARTBREAK

The truth is this: things do not happen the way we imagined them to,
and they rarely ever happen the way we write about them.

I wanted to glorify the heartbreak, and tell everyone a sensational story
where the princess conquers the wicked dragon.

In my story, I slay the dragon.

The writer in me wanted it to be a source of inspiration,
a saga of valor. A tale of triumph.

I was no princess, though, and you were no dragon.
The real story goes something like this:

I raised my sword to kill you,
but plunged it into my own chest instead.

THE UNATTENDED HEART

Love is a real, breathing, living thing
—is it not? It must be tended to, nurtured.

You were a fool to believe it could thrive
alone in a dark room, somewhere, while you were
nowhere to be found.

Where were you?

Don't you know that living things eventually rot
if they are left unattended?

THE REAL ME

I wished for so long for someone to see me for
who I really was, but I fear you saw too much.
I let you in too close;
you held up a mirror and I abhorred the person
who stared back at me.
I wonder,
do we really want someone to see us as we are,
or as we want to be?
I let you in too close and
you ended up on another side of me.

THE HIDDEN SUITCASE

On the most mundane days,
there is a longing for something more—
for a glimpse into another life,
something beyond my own.

What do you call the overwhelming desire
to escape your life?
A vacation or a slow suicide?
Who, in their right mind, hasn't imagined fleeing it all?
We all have a packed suitcase
hidden in the darkest corners of our minds.

THE SCULPTOR

You marvel at what you have created out of me with your cruelty
with a wild fascination, as if you are a sculptor sent by god
to carve a woman out of me.

This was a necessary pain, you say.

I did not know it back then.
I was in a rush to grow up.

Womanhood is a breeding ground for suffering,
this much I now understand.

*Little girls should be allowed to remain little girls
for as long as possible.*

THE STORM

On my best days
I am half-woman, half-storm.

On my worst days,
I am unable to stop the storm
from swallowing me whole.

THE IMMIGRANT DREAM

I have watched the most brilliant and beautiful minds
cower behind the walls of their accents.

I have seen a surgeon from Pakistan
hand me coffee through a Tim Hortons drive-thru window.

Engineers from Egypt and teachers from the Philippines
navigate truckloads of goods across the country.

That is the essence of immigrants:
they grow up and pursue their dreams,
just like the rest of us.
But they have mastered the art
of forging new lives along the way.
They recalibrate for survival,
sacrificing their dreams for the sake of their children.

In their resilience, a strength
that their children often take for granted.

WHERE ARE YOU FROM

has always been an uncomfortable question for me.

They are looking for a simple answer;
(I do not have one).
No one ever asks for a political answer;
(my existence is political).

Are you Indian? they will ask.
No, but home is north of India. Panjab.
Is that not a part of India?
I pause and think about it. *Not in the ways that matter.*

THE VISITOR

The past comes back to visit me, occasionally,
as if it is a memory from another lifetime.

It must have been another lifetime.

Too much time has passed.
Too much has changed.

MARATHONS

He tells me I am good at running,
that I move as if I can outrun pain,
as if I have ever been successful.
(I have not.)

He says running makes me weak,
but would a weak person be able
to run this long?
(I think not.)

My lungs have adapted to carrying me
for miles, but at some point or another
they beg me to stop.
(I do not.)

When I am convinced that I have
traveled far enough, I wait for the ache
to leave my body.
(It does not, it never does.)

GENDER ROLES

I tell him he will never understand
the pain of a woman,
nor how to bleed as I must.

He tells me I will never understand
the ways in which he is not allowed to hurt.

TO BE A WOMAN

This is what I know so far about
being a woman. You stay quiet. The
thoughts are very loud, so you put
pen to paper. Your food is always
cold because you eat last. You bleed
and tell no one about it. Feel rage
but silence it. This is not the time or place
to create a scene. You bleed some
more. Your father gives your hand to
a man. He is a good man, but he does
not know. He does not know of the
rage inside you. He says he would
burn for you. How do you tell him
that you are the fire?

FROM PANJAB TO PALESTINE

There has always been a mother
who cradles her baby for the first time.
But amidst the desecration
of sacred places and saintly souls,
you will find the mother
who holds hers for the last time.

The child she carried so lovingly
for months,
the one who had daily conversations with god,
was fated to enter this world
only to depart so soon.

So, I ask you:
Should we weep for the children
who leave this world too early,
or should we sigh in relief instead?

THE DOLI

On the day I left behind
all the younger versions of myself,
there was laughter and music in the air
and no time for me to tend to them.

I heard the whispers of my childhood among
the giddha and boliyaan.

It is deafening to sit quietly in the only place you
have ever known to be home.

I willed myself not to shed a tear
when the time came to say goodbye,
but there is no dam that can hold back a river of grief
that has been anticipated for years.

I could not allow myself another glance back as
I walked away.

If I had looked
I would never have been able to leave.

CHILD OF IMMIGRANTS' GUILT

My immigrant parents don't know how to take vacations.
There was no such thing as a "me day" for them when I was growing up.
Every single day was a promise to make it to the next,
to provide so their children might thrive someday.
No days off. No sick days. They would take a Tylenol,
accompanied by some desi remedy, and tough it out at work.

Now that I'm grown, my parents still struggle to spend on themselves.
My father wears the same shirts from fifteen years ago,
frowning when we buy him brand-name ones for his birthday.
My mother hesitates to spend a dime on herself.

I am the same age my mother was when she immigrated
from Panjab to Canada. I know her heart must have craved more than this.
Even with everything I have, my heart sometimes craves more.
I wish to give my parents the world,
but I know they wouldn't know what to do with it;
they'd give it back to me.

I want to ask them if it was worth it,
but I lack the courage. Instead, I spend my days
encouraging them to indulge in themselves—
my version of an apology they never wanted or needed.

CHILD OF IMMIGRANTS' GUILT II

When someone gives you a gift,
offers their whole life,
do you do them a disservice
by apologizing?

Dear Mother, I must confess:
On some days, I struggle to meet your eyes.

You left home for a new land,
but the weight of my guilt for your sorrows
devours my gratitude.

Father, sit with me,
and tell me this country has given you
more than it has taken away.

Would you do it all over again

knowing what you know now?

Tell me that I was worth it all.

MY FATHER'S ACCENT

is enough to make you wrinkle your nose
in disgust.

But you have never had to balance
a second language on your tongue,
and even if you think you could,

remember that my mother tongue
makes sounds
that leave English at a loss for letters.

WHO WAS I MADE FOR?

The world likes to tell me that I belong wholly to myself,
but I have come to think that I have been lied to:
nobody belongs to themselves!
Except maybe men, of course.

So, whose am I?
Am I not the property of the mother
whose womb I kicked for months?
Perhaps I am my father's,
and then he transferred me over to another
by giving him my hand?

The urge to know is for a perfectly simple reason:

I want to burn the world to the ground
and I want to know who will still claim me once I do.

TRAUMA ANNIVERSARY

February comes around, again,
and I hope someone will reach out
and tell me they remember, too.

If not,
I hope they will at least say my name out loud.
(I do not know who I am if no one is calling for me.)

It is February, again.

What a burden it is to be the only one who remembers.

THE ENDURING

When I was a child, I would watch
my maa flip roti on the hot pan
with her bare hands.

I stood there, clutching a spatula, stunned.

"Doesn't that burn your hands?"

She would always laugh. "It used to,
but I don't feel it anymore."

Now I wonder how many hot pans
she encountered in her life,
and how much she endured,
before she realized it no longer hurt.
Or is that something one decides one day?

I question if I will ever be half the woman she is,
or if I will always rely on the spatula.
Was I meant to endure the heat of hot pans?

MIGRATION

You tell me you always leave
due to necessity,
like a bird migrating south
for the winter.

I let you back in every single time.

Surely, one day I will get it.

Today is not that day.

THE UNSAID GOODBYE

There was a final day my siblings and I all spent under the same roof, and I didn't even realize it.

Perhaps we would have celebrated it better. We could have taken pictures together to preserve the memory. Maybe we could have hugged each other. Some sort of touch, at least.

Alas, we did not. There were wedding preparations to be done and clothes to be packed and new homes to move into. Our goodbyes must have gotten lost in the hustle and bustle of it all, but maybe this is the best way it could have happened.

Imagine if we had slowed down that day. Imagine we had acknowledged the gravity of the situation, that this was our last day together and life was changing, and we were walking into the unknown. Imagine we came to the realization that the person we saw every single day, we would now see every few weeks or months or years.

Who can move on from a realization like that?

NO LONGER FRIENDS

There were days when I would forget we were no longer friends.
I would wake up with something to tell you, and go to sleep that night
swallowing hundreds of unsaid words.

I became a collection of the things I never told you.

PITY

I look to you for understanding,
some sort of sign that you know what
I have had to endure,

but all you can offer me is your pity,
a soft look of sympathy,

and this is how I know I am broken beyond repair.

AFTER THE HEALING

Nobody talks about what happens after the healing.

Some days, I feel empty without the misery.
There is nothing to hold on to.
There is nothing to fall back on.
There is no one to blame.

Nothing but a feeling of dullness that lingers
before I decide what to do next with my life.

I have healed, I say, *now what?*

No one replies. I lost my only companion. I am alone.

MAYBE

Maybe my misery did not have to take on the form of a poem
(but it stuck around too long, and I did not know what else to do with it).

THE HURTING

I know in my heart of hearts
that you did not mean to be so cruel to me
(you were hurting),

but it does not make it any easier to look back on.

You could have blessed me with a moment of kindness,
a glimpse of mercy
(I was hurting, too).

WHAT IS HOME?

Defining it is like working on the mathematical question
my college professor writes out on a board.

I get to work and realize home is split
and the equations on either side of the border
are not equal.

Home is division, I have gathered,
across people,
across land,
across hearts.

What is home?

It is like a mathematical equation, we insist.
It can be solved.

Somewhere in Panjab,
a mother cries softly
for a son who never returned,

and the whole equation falls apart.

FALLING

Alas,
if only the poets and romantics had taught me
how to climb out of love.

Instead, they spoke only of how to
fall
in—

how to dig yourself so deep
that you can no longer find your way out,

not to realize you've dug your own grave
until it's too late.

WHEN LOVE CALLS

My mother ends every call
by telling me she loves me.

I say it back,
but it almost chokes in the lump in my throat,
struggling to escape my lips.

I don't know if I've lost something inside me
or if it was taken away.

Is love something you grow into,
or something you grow out of?

THE MISCARRIAGE

Pregnancy transforms us into mothers,
but the loss made an infant of me—

a fully grown woman who clutched her womb
and cried out like a baby for her own mother.

My womb is now empty,

my arms are still empty,

but I am still stuck as a mother.

REVOLVING DOOR

I allowed him to step out
and step right in
as if I was a revolving door
and not a woman once made of walls.

THE DOLI II

It feels like one day
I woke up
and my childhood had come to an end.

I buried my adolescence
deep within my heart,
and walked out of my father's house
as a bride.

OCCUPIED

I do not know where my grief ends
and where my healing begins.

I hold them both inside me,
frequently mistaking one for the other.

My whole life has become an untangling of the two
but I don't mind.

It keeps me busy.

PART 2

Homecoming

CONVERSATIONS WITH MY GURU

Japji Sahib
The sun rises.
I rise —
you call for me
and we sit together.

The day has begun.

Jaap Sahib
You offer me words that carry
more strength
than this body has ever known.

Tav Parsaad Savaiye
I realize there is no ritual
that will bring me to you.
There is only love.

Chaupai Sahib
I tell you this world is
a terrible place.

You smile because
you already know.
Why else would you have given me
this protection?

Anand Sahib
I always ask for happiness
in some shape or form

but you remind me there is bliss —
a pure happiness
still waiting to be felt.

Rehraas Sahib
The day has been long;
my body aches,
my mind aches,

and when we sit together
I realize
my soul has been aching, too.

Kirtan Sohila
The moon and the stars
join in, sometimes.

A lot of things haunt my mind,
but tonight they cannot
penetrate my dreams.

You are here, after all.

MEMORIALS

Today,
I plant flowers in all the spaces
you no longer occupy

because sometimes,
grieving cannot begin
without a memorial.

REINCARNATION

Some days,
I wish to disappear.

I attempt to diminish my existence
by making myself smaller,
but my soul suffocates inside my body,
thrashing as if it wishes to escape.

I wonder:
if no one is affected by my presence
or my absence,
do I still have the right to say that I am alive?

I fantasize about shrinking
down to the size of
an ant.

But you remind me
that ants matter, too,
and pull me from drowning
in my own shame.

It is your gaze,
more than anything,
that makes me feel glad to be here.

One look from you
is enough.

A thousand words pour out of me,
as if I am a river

frantically looking for the ocean.

Lifetime after lifetime
(as an ant, as the river),
I will search for you until I find you.

SPOILED FRUIT

Mother,
do not raise me
with the thought of
giving me away.

I
am not your burden
of unwanted fruit
that must be raised
until I ripen.

I
was not made to just
fill the stomachs
of generations
whilst I starve.

Mother,
allow me to grow
and do not worry
about spoiled fruit.

AN ORDINARY THING

I want my existence
to be a soft gesture,
a common thing.

I ask you, dear god,
grant me a simple life—
where I am seen, but not analyzed,
heard, but not misinterpreted.

Allow me to bleed, if I must,
to birth, if I desire,
to grow,
to dance,
to pray,
to break,
and to heal—

as if I am an ordinary person
doing ordinary things.

POSSESSION

If he tells you
he owns you—
if he says,
you are mine,
as if you were some ordinary object—

remember,
you are the ocean,
a force no one can lay claim to.

You are the sky,
vast and beautiful,
and what human
could ever master you?

DEAR BROWN GIRL,

why do you despise your nose?
Your great-great-great grandmother had the same one.
Though no one remembers her name,
you keep her memory alive,
wearing that nose every single day.

Why do you underestimate your dark, brown eyes?
They are the same deep pools
your mother saw her reflection in
as she lovingly lined them with kohl.
Your eyes are globes,
worlds of their own,
drinking in the vibrant hues of your life.

Why do you feel uncomfortable in your brown skin?
It is the result of a deep love affair with the sun—
a bond that cannot be broken.
You carry its warmth with you everywhere.
Each morning,
look in the mirror and realize:
the biggest star in the solar system looks back at you.

So discover the warmth within you,
and make a home out of it.

VISITING MY INNER CHILD

For years,
I ignored the voice of the little girl inside me—
but today, I let down my walls,
approach her cautiously,
and let her gleefully take me by the hand.

We walk together for what feels like days,
through flowered valleys,
among fairies and unicorns.
I am reminded of how much I used to dream,
of the innocence I once carried—
how it used to be
before it was taken away.

She asks me why
I do not visit more often,
and I do not know what to say.
How do I tell her
that it is hard to look at her for too long
without remembering the hurt?

She is just a child.
I was just a child.

She combs my hair,
paints my nails,
and tells me her dreams.
I promise I will try my best
to fulfill them.

She is content.

I bid her farewell
with a promise to return soon.
Then, I come home, remember all the things

that she will have to endure soon,
and cry myself to sleep.

THE WEIGHT OF MEMORY

You say:
Don't forget me—
which is to say
the forgetting is inevitable.

The human heart is like a bee,
moving from one flower to the next.
The reminder to not forget
becomes a prayer to god, my love—
nobody does it enough anymore.

Say: *Remember me*, instead—
which is to say:
How could we ever forget?

Move through life, and no matter
what flower you happen upon,
recall that I existed,
that I was here.

I require no daily worship—
just a momentary thought,
every once in a while.

LONG DISTANCE

There were miles and miles that separated us,

but the space between us was never empty.

(this is where we went to seek god).

CHILD OF GURU GOBIND SINGH

How can I ever think I am worth nothing

when you gave up four diamonds

and felt no loss because

you still had me.

ODE TO PHULKARI

The joy always comes in colors.

Some days I am a blank canvas
or a faded photograph.

But today, my love,
I am a *phulkari*.

HOW TO LOVE

I love being near bodies of water
but I never learned how to swim.

I could sit by the ocean for days,
surrounded by the sounds of waves,
but if they pulled me in
I would not be able to get away.

This is how I have always loved;
I do not know another way to love.

FALLING

I,
a tsu-
nami of a
woman, fell
like raindrops
for you

HEALING FEELS LIKE THIS

A good day followed by an okay day,

followed by three consecutive bad days,

and then another good day;

which is to say that good days will always be nearby;

which is to say that okay days might also be good days;

which is to say that the bad days will eventually end;

which is to accept that they might come back;

which is to say that I will be just fine either way.

ARRANGED LOVE STORY

I do not know if I was a product of true love.
You see, I have never quite found the courage to ask.
I am unsure if my bones were made
to bear the weight of the answer.

But I do know I am made of sacrifice,
of mutual understanding,
of handwritten letters
that crossed oceans to reach aching hands.

I am the mother who gave birth alone
in a new country.
I am the father who left the comforts
and familiarity of Panjab.

I am the sacrifices and compromises
they made along the way.

At first glance, it may not resemble a typical romance,
but perhaps it is truer than any love story ever written.

MY PARENTS WERE CHILDREN ONCE, TOO

It is hard to imagine my father
without his tough, weathered exterior,
but I remind myself he must have been soft
at some point or another. Born into this world,
the same as I was,
he, too, must have had questions
about the universe.

It is even harder to picture my maa as a child.
Why? I do not know.
I feel myself growing into another version of her,
my own childhood slipping away.
Perhaps we force womanhood onto our girls too quickly,
perhaps we mature too fast
because we must.

I close my eyes and imagine a little girl
growing up in a village in Panjab.
Is she happy with her life?
Does she look in the mirror
and like the face that looks back?
Does she ever dream of running away?

Maa shows me a faded, black-and-white photograph
of herself from a distant time.
In it stands a little Panjabi girl
with a face like mine.
I burn that image into my mind.
She was once a child, too.

THE MOTHER OF A FREEDOM FIGHTER

A mother carries a force of a son inside her
and that son cries for freedom as soon as he is born.

She imagines a future full of success for him,
an accomplished career, perhaps,
but he favors an AK-47, instead.

She dreams of a beautiful wedding for her boy,
but he gets married to the struggle.

A mother carries a force of a son inside her,
unaware that he will spend the rest of his life
inside a jail cell, and all she will have to hold on to
are the metal confines that keep him away from her.

BANDI SINGHS

I often wonder what it means to give your life for another.
I always envisioned it to look like taking a bullet for someone.
Or pushing them out of the way and letting the car hit you instead.

But sometimes, it looks like sitting in a jail cell, forgotten.

Sometimes, it looks like taking on the pain of your people,
even though they are not aware that a wound even exists.

Numb. Sedated. Ignorant. Asleep.
     Whatever they may be, they are your people, after all.
     So, you sit and you pray and you continue giving your life
     for them every single day.

NICKNAMES

He does not call me by my name
and this is an intimacy, in itself.

STARGAZING

I do not know how much of the hurt remains.
I wish there were a way to look inside
and see how much I have healed.
I would love to have it quantified,
shown to me as a graph—

percentages,
statistics,
even a pie chart would do.

I would project it onto the night sky
and show you while you held my hand.

Together, we would gaze in amazement
at constellations of healing.

"This is exactly where it hurts,"
I'd say, pointing above.
"This is exactly how much."

You would nod and hold me close,
and I would sigh in relief,
finally understood.

BITTERSWEET BEGINNINGS

They say once your siblings have children,
you are no longer their closest family.

As the sibling who just had her first child,
among the anticipation and pure joy,
allow me a moment to mourn what was.

Picture this: we are young again and
our dreams have not yet changed because
life has not yet changed.
We all still live under the same roof, and a future where
we do not live together does not even seem possible.

Alas, no one stays young forever.
No one stays home forever.

YOU

In every lifetime, it is you.

In every universe,
you.

Even in death.

It is you in every single way
the mortal mind can think of
to come back to this moment.

If I find a way,
it is through you.

If I find a way,
it will be to you.

BLEEDING FOR HOME

Home, they say,
is what your ancestors bled for.

How did my people leave without looking back?
(Hearts full of hope.)

Why do we return?
(Hearts full of longing.)

Someone bled for this homeland, it is said,
and I swear I can hear Panjab wail.

Come home, she calls.
Now, I bleed for you, too.

WHAT IS LOVE?

If love is simply about leaving a lasting impact

on another soul

then I suppose you did love me

in your own way.

PRAYING IN POETRY

Even the simplest of persons
can put together the most heart-wrenching prayer
when she is down on her knees on the ground!

There is a certain poetry to the struggle, is there not?
A kind of beauty in the suffering.

Oh, my mind, do not take pride in your art
       — these are just words pulled out of you by god.

DEFORESTATION

threatens to consume my entire being.

A layer of hair softly covers me,
yet they require smooth, hairless skin
to construct their million-dollar projects—
sky-high towers of insecurities,
reaching up to an unattainable standard.

It's tempting to sell my body
to the machines and corporations
promising me glamour.

But where would the birds sing
if nature could not thrive?

How would I face myself
if I tore down my own home?

THE ART OF HAIR OILING

This is how my mother and I hold on to each other:
She, with her gentle touch, applies coconut oil
to all the places that hurt. The oil melts
in her rugged hands, yet nothing can be softer
than the way she handles me.

She plaits my hair into a braid, weaving her pain
in and out, and I try my best to carry her grief
with the same tenderness. We sit in silence,
hit with a loud reminder:

We don't touch each other often enough,
don't embrace as we once did.
Instead of asking for a hug,
I offer to oil her hair in return.

I am met with an ocean of grays and whites.

I keep forgetting that we are running out of time.

FINAL WORDS

The problem with cremation is
that you don't always get a tombstone
with an inscription.

There are no final words that sum up your life
to passing-by strangers.

So, dedicate a park bench to me when I die
and make sure his name is beside mine.

I was here, I loved him, and he loved me, too.

That is all I want to be remembered for.

THIS IS NOT A LOVE POEM OR AN APOLOGY

You held / with so much softness / all my pain /

gently lulled / my demons into such a slumber/ I forgot they were there /

the hurt / can only hibernate / for so long /

I am ashamed that I left / sorry for the hurt / you must know this /

I left because I had to / I left so I could return / only to return

THE BECOMING

I ask my maa,
Is it harder to be a wife
or a mother?

She tells me
to be a wife,
a woman leaves her homeland
to be a mother,
she must become the homeland.

Tell me, Maa, what is more painful,
leaving or becoming?

The pain of leaving ends,
sometimes,
she says,
but the becoming does not.

ACCEPTANCE

She haunts me,
the person I thought I was going to be,
but how long can you spend worshipping
the person you could have been
before you start neglecting yourself?

In another lifetime,
I dream of the life I am living now.
Certainly, it is time to embrace what I have become.

NEW SKIN

I have shed so many layers of myself since we last spoke

I am no longer a person you have touched

I am no longer a person you know

NOSTALGIA AND ROSE-COLORED GLASSES

I held on to the past the way one might hold on to a newborn child. I nurtured it, looked at it fondly, and desired it to stay that way forever. Unchanged. I held on so tightly to the only proof that happiness had existed at one point in my life, but how could I have forgotten that even memories grow up? That nostalgia is a living, breathing thing that is forever evolving and changing. The further back the memory, the fonder it became. If I could have just let go of the past, I might have realized that it was not as great as I made it out to be. If I had made room for the present, if I had even allowed myself to think about the future, I would have recognized the past for what it was: comfortable. Simply comfortable.

MY DAD CUTS FRUIT FOR ME

Where my parents come from
the men do not lift a finger in the kitchen,
but my dad cuts fruit for me.

My people prefer to have sons
over daughters,
but my dad cuts fruit for me.

Panjabi dads are supposed to be
cold and removed from their daughters,
but my dad cuts fruit for me.

Daughters are going to leave one day
and go to their real homes,
but my dad cuts fruit for me.

PREGNANCY

I have become a home for nine months.
It is terrifying in the same breath that it is beautiful.

I am a home,
a pathway into this world.

There is so much beauty in becoming;
there is so much violence in becoming.

AT THE THOUGHT OF CHILDBIRTH

What do I name this torment that my flesh must learn
before I am united with you?

A biological necessity, perhaps,
or a lesson.

Will I be molded into a mother
with every contraction,
carved into a nurturing being
with every instance of physical pain?

Or does that begin when my skin finally meets yours?

TO BECOME A MOTHER

is to hold all past versions of yourself
while gently letting them go.

It is to recall what it means to be a child,
yet grow up and cease acting like one.

It is to remember the angst of adolescence,
knowing that it does not last forever.

To become a mother
is to release your past
without ever forgetting it existed.

LABOR PAINS

I housed the pain inside of me for months and
(unbeknownst to me)
it grew until I could hide it no longer.

My mother always taught me
that letting go is hardest when
you wait too long.

So, brace yourself,
close your eyes,
remember how to breathe.

Releasing the trauma
is like
giving birth.   It hurts
and then it doesn't.

GROWING PAINS

He thinks I have outgrown him, so
I remind him that my own body
has always pushed me out to make
space for others. How I have
exhausted my lungs and bent my
spine. Broken my back over and
over again, without keeping record
of what love has cost me. If this
is what love is supposed to look
like, I have given it all away and
left none for myself. So, when he
accuses me of being distant, I tell
him that I am not outgrowing him.
I am just finally growing into myself.

TO MY CHILDREN

I will try my best
to store my sadness
where you can never find it—
beneath a loose floorboard,
or in a safe with a code
you will never know.

What I'm trying to say is
I hope you never come across it.
It won't be in the utensil drawer,
or the bathroom sink,
or in your bed with you,
keeping you awake at night.

UNSAID PRAYER

I have made many pleas to god in my lifetime.
I remember days when I knelt down

and begged.

There is no way I could have found the right words
to ask for someone like you—
the words to describe you do not exist.

You are my unsaid prayer.

MOTHER TONGUE

When you speak to me in my maa boli,
in my mother tongue,
I can feel the ache we share between us for a land
blessed by the feet of saints and
baptized by the blood of warriors.

When I respond back to you, it drips off my tongue
like sweet honey.

Come, friend,
let us never stop conversing.

SPRINGTIME

Winter bids farewell and
the sun finally hits my skin
and I remember
that I am a living thing
among the flowers and plants and trees
and not the ghost I made myself out to be.

I open my windows
for the first time in months
and hear the birds excitedly singing,
Wake up, Vaisakhi is coming!

THE HEALING

Suddenly, in the middle of your everyday routine, you realize that you have healed. It does not always take a happy moment to come to this conclusion; sometimes you are doing the most ordinary thing, and the realization hits you hard. The past is not forgotten but it does not weigh you down anymore. You do not think about it every day—in fact, you have not thought about it for a long time now. You made some mistakes and carried that guilt with you, but you figured out a way to forgive yourself. You are alive, you are thriving, and best of all, you are content.

FARMER'S PROTEST

An elder does not join a revolution
at his old age,
does not trade in a house
for the cold streets of Delhi,
does not sacrifice his last few years
for generations that don't yet exist
without reason.

He knows the value of an honest living,
of the backbreaking labor
and unwavering patience required
to nurture creation.

This knowledge makes him formidable.
This knowledge wins wars.

A TRIBUTE TO DEEP SIDHU

Panjab, the shared heart of all its people.

You taught me how to carry that heart
outside of my body
with such grace.

The whole world could turn against me
and I would remain steadfast,

meditating on the rhythm of that beating heart
until the very last breath.

Death itself could come get me,
but that heart would never stop beating.

INHERITANCE

I don't like wearing jewelry but
my maa is always finding excuses to buy me gold.
She tells me it is a good investment, even if it lays
around in a bank collecting dust for years.
One day, you will use it.
I roll my eyes, as usual. Her look softens.
I just want to give you something you can
remember me by when I am gone.
With a lump in my throat, I nod.

I think of all the Panjabi women who came
before me. Hiding their gold under mattresses
and locking it in *Godrej* safes. Passing it down to
their daughters and sending them off to their
in-laws with some financial security.

I hope they were remembered.
I never want to forget.

INHERITED TRAUMA

I know you wish you could have kept your mother safe
from the things she does not talk about
(then maybe she never would have passed them on to you),
but I promise you,
she did not envision angry outbursts and broken dishes
when she held you in her arms for the first time.

That is the funny thing about trauma;
it always manages to seep into parts of our lives
and hurt those that we love the most.

I know you wish you could go back
and shield her from the pain,
but I want you to focus on healing yourself
so you can move forward
and keep your children safe instead.

IN THE DREAM I ONCE HAD

my people are free.

Our crops are thriving.
Kirtan flows out of every loudspeaker.
Our language flourishes.
Our sons and daughters are safe.
And no one feels compelled to hop on a plane
and leave it all behind in the search for something better.

There can be nothing better.

THE PASSAGE OF TIME

I found my first white hair, the other day,
a curious little strand among all the black,
almost as if it was waiting for me to find it.

I wasn't looking for it, really,
so it came as a surprise.

My maa tells me it's because of the products I use in my hair,
and not a result of aging.

Back in Panjab, we used to wash our hair with dahi, yogurt.
It was all natural.

I can't help but laugh to myself at her assurances
that I am not aging
(I try to convince myself often
that she is not aging, either).

Time catches up with all of us eventually,
this much I know:

I am tired of trying to run away from it.

IF I SHOULD HAVE A SON

I will pour into him stories of a lineage
full to the brim with sacrifice
and remind him that the blood of warriors
runs through his veins.

I will teach him about the strength it takes
to remain resilient in the face of injustice,

to have everything taken away from you
and still find a way to remain grateful.

If I should have a son,

I will teach him about the art of flourishing
in a world that is meant to break him,
and pray he will come to me if he does fall apart.

A REMINDER ABOUT HEALING

I know that it feels like it is going to hurt forever, but I promise that it won't. We, humans, have this tendency to forget that all things pass, and so does the pain. It is hard, though, when you are right in the thick of it, to start thinking about healing, but this is what will alleviate the suffering.

Healing is a funny thing; sometimes you don't even know you are experiencing it, until one day, you wake up and everything feels okay.

So, let your loved ones in and share as much of your pain as you can. Talk to god, dance in the rain, and watch as many sunsets as you can.

Yes, you will carry the sadness with you throughout all of it, but one day it will not feel as heavy anymore.

HAPPILY, EVER AFTER

I want you to know that there is no shame
in wanting to be with another person.
To want to open yourself up to them
and to give them everything you can.
To plan a lifetime with them
and to make a family out of them.
There is no shame in wanting a hand to hold.
A bed to share. There is no shame in that, at all.

ACKNOWLEDGMENTS

Above all, my deepest gratitude goes to my family and friends. Your unwavering love and support have been the foundation of this journey, and without you, this book would never have come to life.

To my husband, Prabhjot Singh—my muse, my editor, and my greatest champion. Your belief in me has been my constant source of strength and inspiration.

A heartfelt thank you to my publishing team at Central Avenue Publishing: Michelle Halket, Beau Adler, and Molly Ringle. Your faith in my words has been a gift, and this book is here because of your belief in my writing.

And finally, to you, dear reader—thank you for picking up this book and giving it a home in your hands and heart.

Harman Kaur, a Panjabi Sikh poet and writer
born and raised in British Columbia, Canada,
now calls the Bay Area, California, home.
Through powerful words, she fearlessly explores
the intricate layers of her identity, exemplified in
her collections, *Phulkari* and *Call Me Home.*

@harmank.aur

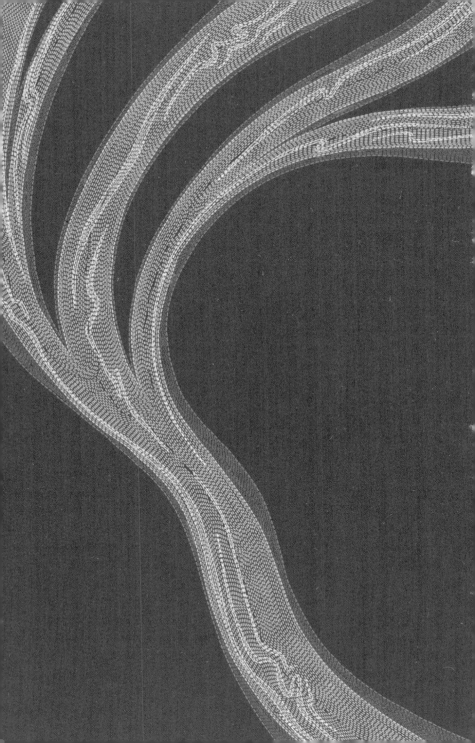